Dear Parent:
Your child's love of reading starts here!

Every child learns to read in a different way and at his or her own speed. Some go back and forth between reading levels and read favorite books again and again. Others read through each level in order. You can help your young reader improve and become more confident by encouraging his or her own interests and abilities. From books your child reads with you to the first books he or she reads alone, there are I Can Read Books for every stage of reading:

SHARED READING
Basic language, word repetition, and whimsical illustrations, ideal for sharing with your emergent reader

BEGINNING READING
Short sentences, familiar words, and simple concepts for children eager to read on their own

READING WITH HELP
Engaging stories, longer sentences, and language play for developing readers

READING ALONE
Complex plots, challenging vocabulary, and high-interest topics for the independent reader

I Can Read Books have introduced children to the joy of reading since 1957. Featuring award-winning authors and illustrators and a fabulous cast of beloved characters, I Can Read Books set the standard for beginning readers.

A lifetime of discovery begins with the magical words "I Can Read!"

Visit www.icanread.com for information
on enriching your child's reading experience.

*To women scientists
around the world.
—S.A.*

*To lovers of nature
and its diversity.
—G.M.*

Picture Credits
Page 31: Chimpanzee in a nest by Cyril Russo copyright © Minden Pictures.
The following photographs are copyright © Getty Images: page 29: Goodall, by Fotos International; Hugo
at age seven, Hulton Archive / Stringer; Goodall in 2010, BERTRAND GUAY/AFP; page 30: Goodall
with a chimp in the Gombe National Park in northern Tanzania, Bettmann; a chimpanzee embraces her
baby, *The Sydney Morning Herald*, Fairfax Media; chimpanzee's foot, Anup Shah/Nature Picture Library;
page 31: Goodall with binoculars and Goodall with chimpanzee from the television special "Miss Goodall
and the World of Chimpanzees," December 22, 1965, Gombe National Park, Tanzania, CBS Photo Archive;
page 31: Goodall with chimpanzee poster, 5/13/1985, Bettmann; Roots & Shoots, Duffy-Marie Arnoult
WireImageCollection.

I Can Read® and I Can Read Book® are trademarks of HarperCollins Publishers.

Library of Congress Control Number: 2019944627
ISBN 978-0-06-243279-7 (trade bdg.)—ISBN 978-0-06-243278-0 (pbk.)

Book design by Marisa Rother
19 20 21 22 23   SCP   10 9 8 7 6 5 4 3 2 1
❖   First Edition

I Can Read!

JANE GOODALL

A Champion of Chimpanzees

by Sarah Albee
pictures by Gustavo Mazali

HARPER
An Imprint of HarperCollinsPublishers

Jane Goodall sat high in a tree
in a rain forest in eastern Africa.
She peered through the thick leaves.

Jane watched some wild chimpanzees.

Her only tools were a pencil,

a notebook, and binoculars.

Jane was twenty-six.

The year was 1960.

Jane had no science training.

She had not even gone to college.

Over the next fifty years,
Jane would learn more about chimps
than anyone else in the world.

Jane had loved animals all her life.

For her second birthday,

Jane got a huge toy chimpanzee.

She carried it everywhere.

When Jane was five, she decided

to watch a hen lay an egg.

She crept into the henhouse.

Five hours later, the hen laid an egg!

Jane's mother couldn't find her.

She was frantic with worry.

But she did not scold her daughter.

She loved Jane's interest in animals.

As Jane grew, she took notes

about pets and farm animals.

Her favorite animal of all

was a dog named Rusty.

He lived at a hotel nearby.

But he spent his days with Jane.

Jane dreamed of going to Africa

to study the animals there.

But she had to earn a living.

At eighteen, she became a secretary.

Then one day Jane got a letter.

It was from an old school friend.

The friend lived in Kenya.

Would Jane like to come for a visit?

Of course she would!

Jane met a famous scientist in Kenya.

His name was Louis Leakey.

He noticed Jane's way with animals.

He offered her a dream job.

Did she want to go to the rain forest

to study wild chimpanzees?

Of course Jane said yes!

For the first two months,

Jane's mother came along to help.

They set up camp in a rain forest,

in a country that would

soon be called Tanzania.

Every day, Jane sat on a hill.

For hours, she watched the chimps.

But they were far in the distance.

They ran when Jane came too close.

Jane tried to remain patient.

She tried not to lose hope.

Some days it poured.

Some days she saw snakes.

Buzzing insects bit her.

Once she was scared by a cougar.

Jane named all the chimps she saw.

There was Flo and Fifi and Olly.

She even named a chimp Leakey.

Then one day a chimp came closer.

Jane had named him David Greybeard.

He showed others not to be afraid.

Gradually, the chimps lost their fear.

They came to visit Jane at her camp.

She gave them bananas to eat.

No one had ever gotten this close

to wild chimpanzees before!

Jane discovered that chimps can feel
angry, sad, lonely, and joyful.
They even have best friends.

One day, Jane saw a chimp make

a tool out of a long stalk of grass.

He poked it into a termite mound.

Then he slurped up the termites.

Before that, people thought

only humans made and used tools.

Another day, Jane discovered
chimps eating meat.
Before that, people thought
chimps ate only plants.

A photographer named Hugo
came to take pictures of Jane.

There was a TV show about Jane.

After that, Jane became famous.

Louis Leakey arranged for Jane

to earn her PhD in England.

Now she would be Dr. Goodall.

Jane and Hugo got married.

A few years later, they had a son.

His name was also Hugo.

Over the years, Jane worked hard.

She started a research center.

She helped many young scientists.

She wrote many books about chimps.

She received many awards.

Jane visited chimps in science labs.

She helped make their lives better.

She worked with zoos
to give chimps more space to play.

She helped take care of baby chimps
whose mothers had died.

When Jane was too old to climb trees
she traveled far and wide.
She gave speeches about chimps.
She helped people find ways
to protect the rain forest.

Jane inspired a new generation
of future scientists
to follow in her footsteps.

Today Jane is famous for her work
with chimpanzees.
But she has also helped protect
living spaces for both people
and animals around the world.
Remember Jane's toy chimpanzee?
She kept it for the rest of her life.

Timeline

1934
Valerie Jane Morris-Goodall is born in London on April 3.

1957
Goodall works for Louis S.B. Leakey at the Nairobi National Museum in Kenya.

1960
Goodall begins observing chimps at Gombe Stream Game Reserve.

1964
Goodall marries Hugo van Lawick, a wild animal photographer.

1965
Goodall earns a PhD from Cambridge University. She establishes the Gombe Stream Research Center.

Hugo at age seven.

1967
Goodall's son, Hugo Eric Louis van Lawick, is born.

Goodall publishes the first of many books about chimpanzees.

1977
The Jane Goodall Institute is created.

1991
Goodall creates a youth organization called Roots & Shoots.

2014
Goodall celebrates her eightieth birthday.

1930
1940
1950
1960
1970
1980
1990
2000
2010

Did you know these facts about chimpanzees?

This female chimp named Fifi is inspecting Goodall curiously.

Each chimpanzee has its own personality. And chimpanzees can feel emotions. Scientists used to think only humans felt happy, sad, angry, or curious.

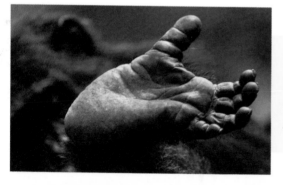

Chimps walk on their front knuckles. Chimps have a big toe that looks like a human thumb. That means they can use their feet to grasp branches and food.

Chimpanzees sleep in trees and make their own nests every night by bending branches.

What was Jane Goodall's life with the chimps like?

It was not easy to study chimps in the hot, hilly rain forest. Often Goodall was drenched in rain. Sometimes she had to crawl on her stomach to make her way through dense trees and vines. Once when she waded into a lake, a six-foot-long snake slithered past her. The air was often thick with mosquitoes and biting insects.

What's in a name?

Before Jane Goodall came to study chimpanzees, most scientists and animal researchers assigned numbers to the animals they studied. Goodall chose to give the chimps names. Some people thought that was unscientific. But Goodall did it her way.

Jane Goodall has received many honors for her work. She has given speeches all over the world, urging people to protect chimpanzees and their environment.

Do you want to know more?

Here are some links you can look up online:

Roots & Shoots

This youth organization has become active in more than 130 countries. Its purpose is to encourage young people to respect and care for their environment, as well as for animals and people.
www.rootsandshoots.org

Jane Goodall Institute

This global organization helps provide funding for animal research. It also helps improve living conditions for people and protects environments.
www.janegoodall.org